Mother's Daughter

Pam Ndumbi

Presentation by *BookLeaf Publishing*

Web: www.bookleafpub.com

E-mail: info@bookleafpub.com

ISBN: 9789357615921

First edition 2022

*Dedicated to all the hard working mothers
out there who haven't been told thank you
in a long time.*

ACKNOWLEDGEMENT

I'd like to thank my mom for always pushing me to choose kindness, see the good in everyone, and keep my faith. To my dad and brother in heaven, I hope you're proud. To my siblings and grandparents, thank you for being patient with me all these years. To anybody else who's ever been kind to me, given me a second chance, or taught me something very valuable, I did not forget you. Thank you.

PREFACE

There are so many things I can't articulate in simple words. Writing is an outlet for me to get all of my feelings out of my mind and onto a page. I want people who are reading this to experience the joys in life, the pain, the lessons, and everything in between.

It's Alright, Child

"It's alright child," I sing to her.
I sing to her; my voice still gruff.
It's 4:00 in the morning,
and her cries murmur like cello strings.
I trudge, trudge to the kitchen,
and put eggs in a frying pan.

It's just me; I've been on my feet.
I'm broken, weary, withdrawn, sunken
she weeps and whimpers.
I hold burnt eggs in my hands.

She looks at me as if to say
"What will you bring for me now?"

I'll Tell You A Bedtime Story

2

There once was a girl who looked very scared.
She saw a big person the size of a bear.
The little girl, small, timid, and weak,
asks the person "will you make a meal out of
me?"
"Why would you think that? Do you have any
kindness to spare?"

I Drew You A Picture

"Mommy, I drew you a picture. It's of you and me at the river, and you're wearing that pink shirt you always wear, and I'm in a nice dress you picked out for me. I'm sitting down on the grass, and you're running because the wind blew my hat away and you're trying to go get it. Do you know why I drew you? My teacher told us to draw our hero, and I drew you. I wanna be just like you when I grow up."

Stop Crying

I hate getting ready in the mornings.
I don't want to go to school.
The kids make fun of my looks,
everyone thinks I'm so uncool.

I hate getting ready in the mornings.
No one will sit with me on the bus.
The kids talk of sleepovers and hangouts,
the seat next to me collects dust.

I hate getting ready in the mornings.
I go to the library to feel safe.
I read Seuss, Munsch, Berenstain, Park.
Wanting an escape.

I hate getting ready in the mornings.
I'll go straight to my room when I'm home
I won't let my mom watch me fold
She'll tell me to stop crying—
She'll tell me the world will swallow me whole.

Empty Kitchen

Who left these dishes in the sink?
"Could it be me?" I start to think.

Roll up my sleeves, let out a sigh,
I wash, rinse, wash, rinse, wash, rinse, cry.

I can't stand on my own two feet,
it's far too much. I'm far too weak.

My frail fingers begin to ache.
They ache, and quake, and flake, and break.

I long to shrink; long to expand,
long for a clean plate in my hand.

Everyone's asleep. I'm still up.
Everyone's sound asleep. I'm up.

Silent Dinner

6

Something wrong at school?
"It was fine. I'm just tired."
Can't get through to her.

I Don't Do Anything Right

I haven't done laundry, she's going to school in stained clothing. The sinks are full with dishes, the toilets haven't been scrubbed, the floors are filthy. I keep missing deadlines to sign permission slips. She asks the lunch ladies for emergency lunches. By the time I get home from work, I can't cook for her. I can't show up for her when she needs me to. One day she'll see it, and one day she'll hate me for it. I felt a tight throat but I have to hold back. I can't let her see me fold when she's used to seeing me tall. I can't be the mom she needs me to be. I don't know what I'm doing. I don't do anything right.

Hi Sweetheart,

If you're reading this, I'm already gone. I know I said I would stop working night shifts, but it's just me taking care of you, and things get out of hand.

If the supermarket is still open, can you please pick up some flour and eggs? I'm going to try to whip you up something special tomorrow aside from the usual bread and butter. Better yet, maybe you can make breakfast tomorrow? These days I don't have strength.

Please don't be mad at me, but I don't think I'll be able to make it to your Parent Teacher Conference tomorrow. I promise though, this weekend I'm all yours. We can go to that nice spot downtown you used to love when you were a little girl.

I'm sorry, there's no dinner for you again. I promise, I'll get it together. I've left $5 on the kitchen counter (or I might've left it somewhere in the living room), maybe you can get something small from McDonald's tonight? You remember how to get there right? Just remember

what I taught you to never talk to strangers and
be safe.

Your mommy loves you so much

Oh and if I accidentally left the stove on again,
please turn it off.

Off to work now, see you in a bit.

Love you,

Mom

Dear Diary,

I want to sympathize with my mom, but she serves me moldy bread and butter for breakfast. She leaves me silly notes on the fridge, but can't even show up for me at school. I wanted her to see me, to really see me.

I have a hope for her that dissipates. it dissipates like she does. I know there's a good mom in there, but I can't help but feel she would've been better off without me.

I want to tell her to stop promising me things, to stop giving me a pittance of an allowance to get crap food because she can't cook to save her life and doesn't remember to turn the stove off. It's pathetic. She's pathetic.

I hate my mom. I hate her. I love her. I hate what she does to me. I don't know.

I Won't Be There

It's daylight.
The morning rays began to seep through my
blinds.
I hear the buzz of the busy streets,
I think of the mailman, the bus drivers, the
parents working a 9-5.
All of them have places to be, goals they haven't
achieved.
Me too, but I lay there motionless.

A nightingale flew to my window,
And sang to me. It sang to me
like it was blind to the impending doom
that surrounds it each day.
I wondered why they still sing
when the world is so cruel.

The doctor said I had three months left.
It will take hold me quicker than that I think,
I won't be there to catch her when she falls,
to see my daughter take on the world.

this–Bogeyman, this Terrifier, this Goblin,
it's stuck on me the way debt clings to a college
student

I can't balance the uneasiness
while trying to pack in as much life as I can.

All I can focus on is that I'm not going to be
there.

The Fig Tree

I used to take my daughter down to the river when she was small. I took her today to feel the same stillness of the water, to embody the same timelessness, and to be able to tell her what she needed to hear. I could feel she wasn't entirely present, but neither was I.

"Mom, I'm scared that when I go to college, I'll change my mind on my career path and have to start all over." "There's nothing wrong with starting over. So long as you're alive, take as many chances as you need."

I got a lump in my throat when I said that. I couldn't tell her what I actually wanted to say.

Instead I spoke of the first time I brought her to the river:

"We raced through the tall weeds, and the wind robbed us of our balance. I told you about the Fig Tree that would one day bear lively fruits and be able to withstand any hardship. Then we watched the stars pencil themselves into the sky."

I stood there staring at the river. I stood still.

"Mom, can we go home? I'm tired"
"Me too."

You're The Reason

You tell me things like "don't you cry"
but why should I not feel my pain?
I wish you weren't my mom sometimes
I wish you wouldn't be so vain.

"You wait until you leave this place,
you'll see how much you needed me."
The nerve to say that to my face,
when all you've been is obsolete.

I don't feel bad for storming out
You don't respect my voice at all
You fill your head with all this doubt
when you're the reason I would fall.

I'll leave this place; I wont turn back
I'll come to get my things and pack.

I'm Sorry I Didn't Tell You

16

Hi sweetie,

I'm at Rocky View Hospital. I'm not feeling
well.
I—I'm sick. I'm sorry I didn't tell you.
Listen, If you don't make it on time, I left a
letter.
It's on my night stand. Read it when you're
ready.
Please just come fast. I need to see you.

Please Call Me Back

Mom, what's happening?
I don't get it, you seemed fine.
Please just call me back.

Her Phantom Follows Me

I lay buried in my mucky, unwashed bed sheets.
A fly fights with the trap placed on my moldy
window
Its buzzing pains me, but I remain still and
anxious,
like a kid awaiting his parents in detention.

I write my final high school diploma today, but
a weight isn't being lifted off of my shoulders.
The weight and I are wrestling, and I crumble
like The House of Usher—
dull, dark, and soundless.

I do once more the dreaded sequence of cram
studying,
trying to regurgitate what little information I had
retained.
The pages of my textbook devour me,
the way winter devours light.

I need my mom.
I feel her more in her absence. Her phantom
follows me
the way I'd follow her in the store to not lose my
way

except now that feeling of loss is stained on me.

I don't know why I ever wanted to grow up.
I don't know what I'm doing. I don't do anything
right.

It Was A Gift

Can I feel bittersweet about Christmas?
I think back to '09 when I was feeble, foolish,
ferocious.
I thought you wanted to ruin my life, mom;
I thought I wanted to be grown.

The morning you woke me to go to the mall,
I wanted to crawl into a cave.
Trying to play it cool wasn't easy,
especially with a mother like you.

I hope you understand why I said I was shopping
alone
when I ran into some kids from school.
"You can hang out with your friends if you
want."
I wish I didn't make you say that.

When you bought me that Christmas sweater,
It was the ugliest thing I'd ever seen.
It was a purple and black monstrosity;
I couldn't understand why you loved it so much.

I didn't want to wear it for the family picture,
so I came downstairs in a dress instead.

"Where's the sweater I bought you the other
day?"
I wish you would've seen the look on your face.

Had I known that shopping trip meant what it
meant for you,
I would've stuck it through; I would have stayed
right there.
I wish that I had worn that sweater that day.
I wished and I wished, and I imagined
what kind of smile would've been on your face.

I went to the mall this morning,
which I haven't done in many years,
but there I saw a line of Christmas sweaters,
and I uncontrollably began to weep.

You really were painfully embarrassing,
but you always made me feel loved.
You live in me, pulse through me, capture me
like an undying song.

I Go Back to the River

Hi mom,

It's been a while.
The flowers here are woeful, wilted, withered.
I used to wake up screaming as a child,
and you'd tell me that nightmares don't last.

This is a nightmare I can't wake up from.
It starts with you walking through the door
and telling me you came back.
You were back, then I'd wake up.

It feels weird to cry. You hated it.
You said the world would swallow me whole,
that there's no room for Glass Roses.

I spent so much time resenting you,
wanting to be unshackled.
I got what I wanted; I realized I was stupid.

I go back to the river, I go back to your words,
you said I'd grow to be mighty like the Fig Tree.
I see you in the stars and the sea.
I feel your warmth flow through me
like an artist's love for creation.

You and I are the same.
I'm sorry I didn't see that before.
I read your letter today.

The Letter

My dearest daughter,

I want to preface by saying you are everything I
could have ever wanted in a daughter and more.

If you're reading this, it means I'm already gone.
I can't imagine what you're feeling right now.
I'm sorry I didn't tell you I was sick…I was
embarrassed. I wanted you to see me strong.
That's what I've wanted your entire life, to be
the mom you created in your head; the one you
used to draw pictures of. I'm not her at all, and
in the coming years, I'll altogether be a familiar
stranger

I never told you how much that day at the river
meant to me. I watched you talk about your
diplomas and how scared you were to go to
college. I was scared too. Scared and proud. A
joyful sadness. I felt my daughter slipping
through my fingers like quicksand, and I was
obsolete.

You'll feel bad. Please don't feel bad. You're
still so young. You're figuring out who you want
to be. We had that in common.

I hurt you and hurt you, and you shed so many
silent quick tears because of me. I was wrong to
make you think that you can't cry in this world.

Cry, scream, shout, then go to bed and try again.
You can't go down with this world. Remember
what I told you—you will have trouble, but take
heart.

Things will be hard, but take heart.

I love you,

Mom